Korean Conversations - Fun Korean Language Practice
Learn Korean Fast Book 3

Allen Williams PhD

Sulseob Jo PhD

PUBLISHED BY:
PowerMeUp Publishing
Copyright © 2012
LearnKoreanFast.com

ISBN 978-4-907477-39-4

The conversations here are all a work of fiction. All characters, names, places and events are the product of the author's imagination or used fictitiously.

____

Table of Contents

Introduction

About the authors

Skip this at your own risk!
All study is not bad. However, much of it is boring, and worse, a waste of time.

This book is neither of those things.

Why waste your time studying boring things or in a boring way? Just because it's the way most everyone is doing things?

This book is for any level of Korean language learner who can read and pronounce Hangul.

This is not a textbook in the usual sense. It is really more of a practice and example book. There are no "lessons" lain out for you, but you may find some notes where further explanation is necessary or just interesting.

Also, it's very unlikely you will ever have any of these conversations word for word in your real life.

In fact, these translations may at times not be exactly what a Korean might say in this situation, but it will be close. The reason is the conversations and sentences were constructed to give the closest of literal translation possibilities. So, there are no idioms, expressions, or analogies here. There are just straightforward sentences.

That may seem an odd statement to make at this point, but if you consider how many possibilities there are for most conversations other than "How are you?" and "I'm fine, and you?" there really are very few practice conversations in any textbook you might actually have word for word. Why not have fun learning some structures of conversation, some interesting and useful phrases, and exploring the language on your own rather than just be taught to parrot some conversations you will never actually have anyway?

These are practice conversations for you to get exposure to the way normal, comfortable conversations occur, and while there are of course a number of ways to translate or say the same thing in any language, the examples chosen are done so in a way to narrow down those choices.

Each conversation is intended to be both practical and interesting to help you to more easily remember the vocabulary. You will also see several short phrases that are repeated throughout various conversations. This will also help you through repetition to learn those phrases more easily by seeing them in context.

Each conversation is between two people who presumably know each other fairly well. This is important to keep in mind for context and for the levels of politeness either used or implied.

In fact, the situation is more helpful in aiding understanding than knowing the vocabulary, so invest a little time into understanding the context of each conversation you meet whether in this text of any other. It will help you to understand better and more quickly.

You will not find a lot of notes or explanations for several reasons. The main reasons being that by looking at the conversations and the translations you should be able to figure out on your own which parts go together, and the more of this connecting and figuring out you do on your own the easier it will be for you both to acquire the language and to remember it.

This also allows you to work at this at many different levels and at the levels that suit or interest you. For example, you might see some parts as simply being useful vocabulary or expressions, while someone else might notice that the sentence structure can be used for other instances by doing simple replacing of either the noun or the verb stem. You might also find that going over the conversations and memorizing them is great for you when you are a beginner, but as you progress, revisiting the conversations and digging deeper into the sentence structures can help you to expand your ability to communicate even more.

The font is intentionally a little large in order to help you to read the hangul characters a little more easily. Until you are really accustomed to the shapes of Korean words, it takes a little extra time to read some of the words, even when they are typed. Larger fonts help you to "look, then say" at a faster more comfortable pace.

Some things to keep in mind as you go through this book:

- Korean language seldom uses the subject in sentences where it is understood. This is true for people or objects. That means there are very few instances where pronouns or "you" are used. "Are you okay?" in Korean roughly translates to "Okay?" more often than not.
- Yes, there are other ways to say what is being said in these conversations. Each translation has been done in order to reduce the amount of time you need to understand what part of the Korean sentence matches its corresponding part in the translated sentences.
- These conversations were originally written and structured in a way to facilitate translation. They are still as natural as possible in both Korean and in translation. While you may not ever (sometimes hopefully never) have need for any of these conversations word for word any phrase you see here is current, appropriate vocabulary.
- Verbs come last. Korean is a verb driven language. Mostly you will see Subject (implied or understood as well) - Object - Verb sentence structures.
- There are many levels of Korean.
    - o 1. Polite levels for speaking to those who are older than you or above your social station.
    - o 2. Moderate levels used to talk to those who are among your peer group.
    - o 3. Low level (sometimes called 'impolite' as classification, and is when used in the wrong settings) used for speaking to someone much lower than your status in age or social position, but also used to show familiarity. This book tries to stick to the middle ground here. No one should be greatly offended by any of the usages here although it is probably not advisable to use them for talking to the president of your college or company.

That said, let's look at several ways you can use and benefit from these conversations.

- You can just read them and practice them alone by reading them aloud or to yourself.
- You can practice them with a partner. The dialogs are divided to separate pages for this.
- You can practice them along with the recordings.
- You can expand the conversations.- a page for notes and changes is included
- Take a look at the sentences and see if there are any pieces you can work out that may even contain new vocabulary.
- Look for phrases and fragments that you can use in various contexts and situations.
- Most of all – have fun!

17. Do you have any pets?

Damin : Do you have any pets?

Dahyeon: I used to have pets.

Damin : Really? What kind?

Dahyeon: When I was very young we had a dog.

Damin : What kind of dog?

Dahyeon: It was a Chihuahua.

Damin : Oh, those are very small!

Dahyeon: He was very cute and fun.

Damin : What other pets have you had?

Dahyeon: I used to have some goldfish.

Damin : Me, too!

Dahyeon: I had to clean their tank every week though, and that wasn't so good.

Damin : Oh, I know. But, they were kind of fun and easy to take care of.

Dahyeon: I only had mine for about a year. My mom said she set them free.

Damin : Ah… Mine died, too.

Dahyeon: Have you had other pets?

Damin : We had a cat, but it mostly just lived with us.

Dahyeon: They are very independent.

Damin : That's true.

Dahyeon: Why the sudden interest in pets?

Damin : Oh, I thought I saw a mouse under your backpack.

Dahyeon: Ahhhhh!!!!

Damin : So, it's not your pet?

17. 반려 동물 키워?

다민 : 반려 동물 키워?

다현 : 전에는 키웠었지.

다민 : 정말? 뭐 키워?

다현 : 아주 어렸을 때는 개를 키웠어.

다민 : 어떤 개였어?

다현 : 치와와.

다민 : 아, 그 아주 조그마한 거!

다현 : 아주 귀엽고 재밌었어.

다민 : 다른 건 뭐 키웠어?

다현 : 금붕어를 좀 키우기도 했고.

다민 : 나도 키웠었어!

다현 : 매주 수조 청소를 해야 했어. 그 점은 별로였어.

다민 : 그래, 그건 그래. 그래도 금붕어를 기르는 건 꽤 재미있기도 하고 돌보기도 쉬워.

다현 : 한 1 년 동안 키웠는데, 어느 날 엄마가 [금붕어는 다 놓아줬다]고 하시더라구.

다민 : 아 ... 내가 키우던 건 죽어 버렸어.

다현 : 또 다른 건?

다민 : 고양이를 키웠었지. 키웠다기보다는 우리와 함께 살았다고 하는게 옳지.

다현 : 고양이는 참 독립적이야.

다민 : 말 그대로야.

다현 : 왜 갑자기 반려 동물에 관심을 갖고 그래?

다민 : 응, 네 가방 밑에서 쥐 새끼 한 마리를 본 것 같아서.

다현 : 어휴~ ~ ~!!

다민 : 아니, 그건 네 애완 동물이 아니었어?

17. 애완 동물 키워?

다민 : 애완 동물 키워?

다현 : ________________________________

다민 : 정말? 어떤 종류?

다현 : ________________________________

다민 : 무슨 종의 개?

다현 : ________________________________

다민 : 아, 그 아주 조그마한 거!

다현 : ________________________________

다민 : 다른 건?

다현 : ________________________________

다민 : 나도 키웠었어!

다현 : ________________________________

다민 : 그래, 그건 그래. 그래도, 금붕어를 기르는 건 꽤 재미있기도 하고 돌보기도 어렵지 않아.

다현 : ________________________________

다민 : 아 ... 내가 키우던 건 죽어 버렸어.

다현 : ________________________________

다민 : 고양이를 키웠었지. 키웠다기보다는 우리와 함께 살았다고 하는게 옳지.

다현 : ________________________________

다민 : 말 그대로야.

다현 : ________________________________

다민 : 응, 네 가방 밑에서 쥐 새끼 한 마리를 본 것 같아서.

다현 : ________________________________

다민 : 그런데 그건 네 애완 동물은 아니지?

17. 애완 동물 키워?

다민 : ____

다현 : 전에는 키웠었지.

다민 : ____

다현 : 아주 어렸을 때는 개를 키웠지.

다민 : ____

다현 : 치와와.

다민 : ____

다현 : 아주 귀엽고 재밌었어.

다민 : ____

다현 : 금붕어도 좀 키웠지.

다민 : ____

다현 : 매주 수조를 청소를 해야 해서, 그건 별로였어.

다민 : ____

다현 : 한 1 년 동안 키웠는데, 어느 날 엄마가 [금붕어는 다 놓아줬다]고 하시더라구.

다민 : ____

다현 : 또 다른 건?

다민 : ____

다현 : 고양이는 참 독립적이지.

다민 : ____

다현 : 왜 갑자기 애완 동물에 관심을 갖고 그래?

다민 : ____

다현 : 어휴~ ~ ~!!

다민 : ____

MY NOTES:

18. How about lunch?

Hyocheol : Hey, how about having lunch together today?

Younghwa: Sure. Sounds good.

Hyocheol : Where shall we go?

Younghwa: umm… that depends…

Hyocheol : Don't worry. Today I'm buying!

Younghwa: Wow, okay! In that case, how about that new restaurant across the street?

Hyocheol : Good idea! I've been wanting to go there.

Younghwa: Are you ready now?

Hyocheol : Yeah, let's go.

Younghwa: Let me get my coat.

Hyocheol : Okay.

Younghwa: (returns) Okay. Let's go.

Hyocheol : I'm starving.

Younghwa: Me, too. You have good timing.

Hyocheol : You're lucky today!

Younghwa: Ha ha! It looks that way.

Hyocheol : uh oh…

Younghwa: What's wrong? Is the restaurant closed?

Hyocheol : uh… no…

Younghwa: What is it then?

Hyocheol : Maybe I left my wallet at home this morning.

Younghwa: What? I can't believe you!

Hyocheol : I didn't do it on purpose! Please believe me!

Younghwa: Really? Okay, today I'll pay.

Hyocheol : Oh? Today is my lucky day!

Younghwa: Next time lunch is on you though.

Hyocheol : Okay. No problem. I won't forget again.

Younghwa: I hope not.

18. 점심 어때?

효철 : 헤이, 오늘 점심 같이 먹으러 갈까?

영화 : 그래. 그 참 좋은 생각이다.

효철 : 어디로 갈까?

영화 : 음 ... 그건 주머니 사정에 따라서 달라지지.

효철 : 걱정 마. 오늘은 내가 사지!

영화 : 우와, 알았어! 그럼, 길 건너편에 새로 생긴 레스토랑은 어때?

효철 : 좋은 생각이야! 나도 거기 가 보고 싶었거든.

영화 : 지금 이대로 나가도 돼?

효철 : 그래, 가자.

영화 : 아, 내 코트 입고 나서.

효철 : 그래, 천천히.

영화. : (돌아 와서) 자. 가자.

효철 : 배가 많이 고프네.

영화 : 나도 배가 많이 고파. 좋은 타이밍에 와 줬어.

효철 : 너 오늘 운이 무지 좋은 거였지!

영화 : 하하! 그런 것 같아.

효철 : 어, 음 ....

영화 : 무슨 일이야? 레스토랑 쉬는 날이야?

효철 : 아 ... 이럴 수가 ...

영화 : 무슨 일인데 그래?

효철 : 내 지갑, 아침에 집에 두고 온 것 같아.

영화 : 뭐라구? 이거 너무 하시는 군!

효철 : 일부러 그런 거 아냐! 믿어 줘!

영화 : 진짜 일부러 그런 건 아니지? 그래, 오늘은 내가 낼께.

효철 : 아? 오늘은 내가 운이 좋은 날이었구나!

영화 : 다음 점심은 네가 사는 거야.

효철 : 그럼. 걱정 마. 그 때는 지갑 가지고 오는 거 안 잊어 버릴게.

영화 : 제발이지 그래 주셔.

18. 점심 어때?

효철 : 안녕, 오늘을 점심 같이 먹으러 갈까?

영화 : ____

효철 : 어디로 갈까?

영화 : ____

효철 : 걱정 마. 오늘은 내가 사지!

영화 : ____

효철 : 좋은 생각이야! 나도 거기 가 보고 싶었거든.

영화 : ____

효철 : 그래, 가자.

영화 : ____

효철 : 그래, 천천히.

영화. : (돌아 와서) _______________________________________

효철 : 배가 많이 고프네.

영화 : ____

효철 : 너 오늘 운이 무지 좋은 거였지!

영화 : ____

효철 : 어, 음 ....

영화 : ____

효철 : 아 ... 이럴 수가 ...

영화 : ____

효철 : 내 지갑, 아침에 집에 두고 온 것 같아.

영화 : ____

효철 : 일부러 그런 거 아냐! 믿어 주지!

영화 : ____

효철 : 아? 오늘은 내가 운이 좋은 날이었구나!

영화 : ____

효철 : 그럼. 걱정 마. 그 때는 안 잊어 버릴게.

영화 : ____

18. 점심 어때?

효철 : _______________________________________

영화 : 그래. 그 참 잘 됐다.

효철 : _______________________________________

영화 : 음 ... 그건 주머니 사정에 따라서 달라지지.

효철 : _______________________________________

영화 : 와, 알았어! 그럼, 길 건너편에 새로 생긴 레스토랑은 어때?

효철 : _______________________________________

영화 : 지금 이대로 나가도 돼?

효철 : _______________________________________

영화 : 아, 내 코트 입고 나서.

효철 : _______________________________________

영화. : (돌아 와서) 자. 가자.

효철 : _______________________________________

영화 : 나도. 좋은 타이밍에 와 줬어.

효철 : _______________________________________

영화 : 하하! 그런 것 같지?

효철 : _______________________________________

영화 : 무슨 일이야? 레스토랑 쉬는 날이야?

효철 : _______________________________________

영화 : 무슨 일인데 그래?

효철 : _______________________________________

영화 : 뭐라구? 정말 너무 하시는 군!

효철 : _______________________________________

영화 : 진짜 일부러 아니지? 그래, 오늘은 내가 낼께.

효철 : _______________________________________

영화 : 다음 점심은 네가 사는 거야.

효철 : _______________________________________

영화 : 제발이지 그러시게.

MY NOTES:

19. Let's go for a walk!

Damin : Today's weather is really nice.

Dahyeon: It is, isn't it?

Damin : Let's go for a walk!

Dahyeon: Okay! Sounds like a good idea.

Damin : Hurray up and get ready.

Dahyeon: Just a moment.

Damin : Come on!

Dahyeon: Let me change into some better clothes for exercising.

Damin : All right.

Dahyeon: Walking is great exercise.

Damin : I think so, too.

Dahyeon: But the right clothes are important.

Damin : I understand. What's that?

Dahyeon: It's a pedometer.

Damin : What's a pedometer?

Dahyeon: It measures the time and number of steps you take while walking.

Damin : Oh, that's useful.

Dahyeon: Yeah. I also have this.

Damin : What's that?

Dahyeon: It's a heart rate monitor.

Damin : Technology is amazing, isn't it?

Dahyeon: It really is. Even these shoes are specially designed for walking, too.

Damin : You have everything you need.

Dahyeon: Just one more thing.

Damin : What's that other thing for?

Dahyeon: Oh, that's for carrying ice cream money.

Damin : Ice cream money?

Dahyeon: Of course! That's where I always walk to.

19. 우리 워킹 가자!

다민 : 오늘 날씨 참 좋다.

다현 : 정말 좋다, 그지?

다민 : 우리 워킹 가자!

다현 : 그래! 좋은 생각이다.

다민 : 서둘러서 준비하고, 응.

다현 : 아 잠깐만.

다민 : 얼른 가!

다현 : 운동하기 편한 옷으로 갈아 입고나서….

다민 : 알았어.

다현 : 워킹은 아주 좋은 운동이야.

다민 : 나도 그렇게 생각해.

다현 : 그런데 운동하기에 적합한 옷도 중요하지.

다민 : 옳아. 그건 뭐야?

다현 : 보수계.

다민 : 보수계가 뭐야?

다현 : 이건 걷는 동안의 우리가 걸은 시간과 보수를 재어 주는 기기야.

다민 : 아, 그것 참 유용하네.

다현 : 그래. 이런 것도 있어.

다민 : 그게 뭔데?

다현 : 심장 박동 모니터.

다민 : 기술 혁신이 놀라워, 그지?

다현 : 정말이야. 이 신발도 워킹을 위해 특별히 설계된 거잖아.

다민 : 필요한 건 다 갖추었네.

다현 : 한가지 더 필요한 거.

다민 : 한가지 더 필요한 거? 그게 뭔데?

다현 : 응, 아이스크림 살 돈 가지고 가는 거.

다민 : 아이스크림 살 돈?

다현 : 그래! 그곳이 내가 늘 하는 워킹의 목적지거든.

19. 우리 워킹 가자!

다민 : 오늘의 날씨가 참 좋다.

다현 : ____

다민 : 우리 워킹 가자!

다현 : ____

다민 : 서둘러서 준비하고, 응.

다현 : ____

다민 : 얼른 가!

다현 : ____

다민 : 알았어.

다현 : ____

다민 : 나도 그렇게 생각해.

다현 : ____

다민 : 옳아. 그건 뭐야?

다현 : ____

다민 : 보수계가 뭐야?

다현 : ____

다민 : 아, 그 참 유용하네.

다현 : ____

다민 : 그게 뭔데?

다현 : ____

다민 : 기술 혁신이 놀라워, 그지?

다현 : ____

다민 : 필요한 건 다 갖추었네.

다현 : ____

다민 : 한가지 더 필요한 거? 그게 뭔데?

다현 : ____

다민 : 아이스크림 살 돈?

다현 : ____

19. 우리 워킹 가자!

다민 : ____

다현 : 정말 좋다, 그지?

다민 : ____

다현 : 그래! 좋은 생각이다.

다민 : ____

다현 : 아 잠깐만.

다민 : ____

다현 : 운동하기에 편한 옷으로 갈아 입고나서….

다민 : ____

다현 : 워킹은 아주 좋은 운동이야.

다민 : ____

다현 : 그런데 운동하기에 적합한 옷도 중요하지.

다민 : ____

다현 : 보수계.

다민 : ____

다현 : 이건 걷는 동안의 우리가 걸은 시간과 보수를 재어 주는 기기야.

다민 : ____

다현 : 그래. 이런 것도 있어.

다민 : ____

다현 : 심장 박동 모니터.

다민 : ____

다현 : 정말이야. 이 신발도 워킹을 위해 특별히 설계된 거잖아.

다민 : ____

다현 : 한가지 더 필요한 거.

다민 : ____

다현 : 응, 아이스크림 살 돈 가지고 가는 거.

다민 : ____

다현 : 그래! 그곳이 내가 늘 하는 워킹의 목적지거든.

20. I like your new apartment.

Dahyeon: This new apartment is really nice.

Damin : Thanks. I'm glad you like it.

Dahyeon: Did you choose these pictures?

Damin : Actually, those were given to me by my old room mate.

Dahyeon: Oh, I see. How about these rugs?

Damin : They're really nice, huh?

Dahyeon: Very nice. Did you choose them?

Damin : Oh, no. They came with the apartment.

Dahyeon: Ah, well, what about the curtains?

Damin : My girlfriend helped me pick those.

Dahyeon: Well, she did a good job.

Damin : I thought so, too.

Dahyeon: Did you choose anything new for your apartment?

Damin : Not really. I'm not good at that kind of thing.

Dahyeon: But it's important because some things about your home show your personality.

Damin : My personality is to let other people choose when it comes to unimportant things.

Dahyeon: Ha ha! What about the living room?

Damin : Oh, yeah! I picked the TV!

Dahyeon: Wow! It's really nice and big!

Damin : Great, right?

Dahyeon: One thing worries me though.

Damin : What's that?

Dahyeon: Well, your bookcase is much smaller than your television…

20. 새 아파트 좋구나.

다현 : 이 새 아파트 정말 좋다.

다민 : 고마워. 맘에 든다니 나도 좋은데.

다현 : 이 그림들 네가 골랐어?

다민 : 실은 그 그림들은 내 이전의 룸 메이트가 준 거야.

다현 : 응, 그랬구나. 이 양탄자는?

다민 : 그거 정말 좋지, 그지?

다현 : 정말 좋은데. 네가 고른 거야?

다민 : 아니, 아니, 그건 아파트에 딸린 거.

다현 : 아, 그럼, 이 커튼은?

다민 : 내 여자 친구가 골라 줬어.

다현 : 음, 멋진 거 고르셨네.

다민 : 나도 그렇게 생각해.

다현 : 아파트 사고 뭔가 네가 새로 고른 거는 없어?

다민 : 아니, 없어. 난 그런 거 잘 못해.

다현 : 하지만 그런 것도 중요한데. 왜 네 집의 물건이라는 게 너의 개성을 나타내 주기도
하잖아.

다민 : 다른 사람들이 우리 집 물건을 고르게 하는 게 내 개성이지. 특히 별로 중요하지 않게
생각되는 것에 대해서는.

다현 : 아, 그렇구나! 거실의 물건들도 다 그래?

다민 : 오, 아니, 아니! TV는 내가 골랐어!

다현 : 와! 이거 정말 멋지고 크다!

다민 : 멋있지, 그지?

다현 : 그런데 한 가지 걱정되는 게 있어.

다민 : 뭔데 그게?

다현 : 글쎄, 너네 책장이 너네 텔레비전보다 훨씬 작다는 거.

20. 새 아파트 좋구나.

다현 : 이 새 아파트 정말 좋다.

다민 : ___________________________________

다현 : 이 그림들 네가 골랐어?

다민 : ___________________________________

다현 : 응, 그랬구나. 이 양탄자는?

다민 : ___________________________________

다현 : 정말 좋은데. 네가 고른 거야?

다민 : ___________________________________

다현 : 아, 그럼, 이 커튼은?

다민 : ___________________________________

다현 : 음, 멋진 거 고르셨네.

다민 : ___________________________________

다현 : 네 아파트 사고 뭔가 새로 네가 고른 거 없어?

다민 : ___________________________________

다현 : 하지만 그런 것도 꽤 중요한데. 왜 네 집의 물건이라는 게 너의 개성을 나타내 주기도
하잖아.

다민 : ___________________________________

다현 : 응, 그렇구나! 거실의 물건들도 다 그래?

다민 : ___________________________________

다현 : 와! 이거 정말 멋있고 크다!

다민 : ___________________________________

다현 : 그런데 한 가지 걱정되는 게 있어.

다민 : ___________________________________

다현 : 글쎄, 너희 집 책장이 텔레비전보다 훨씬 작다는 거지.

20. 새 아파트 좋구나.

다현 : _______________________________________

다민 : 고마워. 맘에 든다니 나도 좋은데.

다현 : _______________________________________

다민 : 실은 그 그림들은 내 이전의 룸 메이트가 준 거야.

다현 : _______________________________________

다민 : 그거 정말 좋지, 그지?

다현 : _______________________________________

다민 : 아니, 아니, 그건 아파트에 딸린 거.

다현 : _______________________________________

다민 : 내 여자 친구가 골라 줬어.

다현 : _______________________________________

다민 : 나도 그렇게 생각해.

다현 : _______________________________________

다민 : 아니, 없어. 난 그런 거 잘 못해.

다현 : _______________________________________

다민 : 내 개성이라는 건, 다른 사람들이 우리 집의 물건을 고르게 하는 거. 그들이 별 일 없이
우리 아파트를 찾아 왔을 때 말야.

다현 : _______________________________________

다민 : 오, 예! TV는 내가 골랐어!

다현 : _______________________________________

다민 : 멋지지, 그지?

다현 : _______________________________________

다민 : 뭔데 그게?

다현 : _______________________________________

18. What's wrong?

Hyocheol: Hey, you look sad. What's up?

Dahyeon : Yeah, it's my new watch.

Hyocheol: The one that is waterproof?

Dahyeon : Yes, and fireproof.

Hyocheol: And isn't it shock proof, too?

Dahyeon : Oh, yes, of course.

Hyocheol: I think you even said it was okay to use even if you were scuba diving.

Dahyeon : That's true even though I have never gone scuba diving.

Hyocheol: But still, it's nice to know how good and strong it is.

Dahyeon : I guess so.

Hyocheol: I also remember you said it was one of the most accurate watches made today.

Dahyeon : That, too.

Hyocheol: So? What happened? Did it break?

Dahyeon : No.

Hyocheol: It stopped working because you got it wet?

Dahyeon : No, not that either.

Hyocheol: Well, it obviously didn't catch on fire, did it?

Dahyeon : No, no, of course not.

Hyocheol: Then what's wrong with it?

Dahyeon : I don't think anything is wrong with it, but I don't know for sure because I lost it!

21. 무슨 일이야?

효철 : 이 봐, 기분이 안 좋아 보이는데. 무슨 일이야?

다현 : 응, 내 새로 산 시계가….

효철 : 그 방수 시계?

다현 : 그래, 불에도 안 타고.

효철 : 그리고 충격 방비도 되는 거였지?

다현 : 어, 그래, 물론 충격 방비도 되는 거였어.

효철 : 스쿠버 다이빙을 할 때 써도 무방하다고 얘기 했던 것 같은데?

다현 : 말 그대로야. 스쿠버 다이빙을 해 본 적은 없지만 말이야.

효철 : 하지만, 그 시계가 얼마나 좋고 견고한 시계인지 안다는 게 좋은 거지.

다현 : 그건 그래.

효철 : 최근에 나오는 시계중에서 가장 정확한 시계 중의 하나라고도 했던 거 같은데?

다현 : 그렇기도 해.

효철 : 그런데? 무슨 일이야? 고장났어?

다현 : 아니, 고장 아냐.

효철 : 그럼 시계가 젖어서 작동이 안 되는 거야?

다현 : 아니, 그것도 아냐.

효철 : 설마 불에 닿아서 안 가는 건 아니겠지, 그지?

다현 : 아니, 아니, 물론 그런 건 아니고.

효철 : 그럼 뭐가 잘못됐다는 거야?

다현 : 시계에 무슨 문제가 있는 건 아닐 거야. 그런데 그 시계, 잃어버렸어. 그러니까 이젠 성능이 괜찮은지도 알 수가 없어.

21. 무슨 일이야?

효철 : 이 봐, 기분이 안 좋아 보이는데. 무슨 일이야?

다현 : ____

효철 : 그 방수 시계?

다현 : ____

효철 : 그리고 충격 방비도 되었었지?

다현 : ____

효철 : 스쿠버 다이빙을 할 때 써도 무방하다고 얘기 했던 것 같은데?

다현 : ____

효철 : 그래도 얼마나 좋고 견고한 시계인지 알고 있다는 게 좋은 거지.

다현 : v

효철 : 최근 만들어지는 시계중에서 가장 정확한 시계 중의 하나라고도 했던 거 같은데?

다현 : ____

효철 : 그런데? 무슨 일이야? 고장났어?

다현 : ____

효철 : 그럼 시계가 젖어서 작동이 안 되는 거야?

다현 : ____

효철 : 설마 불에 던져서 안 가는 건 아니겠지, 그지?

다현 : ____

효철 : 그럼 뭐가 잘못된 거야?

다현 : ____

21. 무슨 일이야?

효철 : ＿＿＿＿＿＿＿＿＿＿＿＿＿＿＿＿＿＿＿＿＿＿＿＿＿＿＿＿＿＿＿＿

다현 : 응, 내 새로 산 시계가….

효철 : ＿＿＿＿＿＿＿＿＿＿＿＿＿＿＿＿＿＿＿＿＿＿＿＿＿＿＿＿＿＿＿＿

다현 : 그래, 불에도 안 타고.

효철 : ＿＿＿＿＿＿＿＿＿＿＿＿＿＿＿＿＿＿＿＿＿＿＿＿＿＿＿＿＿＿＿＿

다현 : 응, 그래, 물론 충격 방비도 되었었지.

효철 : ＿＿＿＿＿＿＿＿＿＿＿＿＿＿＿＿＿＿＿＿＿＿＿＿＿＿＿＿＿＿＿＿

다현 : 말 그대로야. 스쿠버 다이빙을 해 본 적은 없지만 말이야.

효철 : ＿＿＿＿＿＿＿＿＿＿＿＿＿＿＿＿＿＿＿＿＿＿＿＿＿＿＿＿＿＿＿＿

다현 : 그렇지 뭐.

효철 : ＿＿＿＿＿＿＿＿＿＿＿＿＿＿＿＿＿＿＿＿＿＿＿＿＿＿＿＿＿＿＿＿

다현 : 그렇기도 해.

효철 : ＿＿＿＿＿＿＿＿＿＿＿＿＿＿＿＿＿＿＿＿＿＿＿＿＿＿＿＿＿＿＿＿

다현 : 아니.

효철 : ＿＿＿＿＿＿＿＿＿＿＿＿＿＿＿＿＿＿＿＿＿＿＿＿＿＿＿＿＿＿＿＿

다현 : 아니, 그것도 아냐.

효철 : ＿＿＿＿＿＿＿＿＿＿＿＿＿＿＿＿＿＿＿＿＿＿＿＿＿＿＿＿＿＿＿＿

다현 : 아니, 아니, 물론 그건 아니고.

효철 : ＿＿＿＿＿＿＿＿＿＿＿＿＿＿＿＿＿＿＿＿＿＿＿＿＿＿＿＿＿＿＿＿

다현 : 시계에 무슨 문제가 있는 건 아닐텐데 잘은 모르겠네. 그런데 그 시계, 잃어버렸지 뭐야.

19. Did you enjoy the movie?

Younghwa: How was the movie last night?

Damin   : Oh, it was really good. You should go see it.

Younghwa: I don't go to the movies very often.

Damin   : Really? Why not? Don't you like movies?

Younghwa: I love movies, but going to the theater is not so good these days.

Damin   : I know sometimes it can be really bad with the prices for tickets.

Younghwa: Food and drinks are pretty expensive, too.

Damin   : That's true. But still, watching a movie in the theater is a different experience from watching at home.

Younghwa: Of course, the big screen, the great sound system, and the atmosphere are better at the theater.

Damin   : Some movies are okay to watch at home, but sometimes you just have to see a movie in a theater.

Younghwa: I agree, but it just takes too much time, and money, and people are talking.

Damin   : I understand, but sometimes it is worth it.

Younghwa: Maybe.

Damin   : What's the last movie you watched in the theater?

Younghwa: "Titanic".

Damin   : Wow! That's a long time ago!

Younghwa: Not really. The 3D version was showing last month. I have pictures on my phone here!

22. 그 영화 재미있었어?

영화 : 어제 밤에 본 영화 어땠어?

다민 : 아, 그거 정말 좋더라. 너도 가서 봐.

영화 : 나는 영화 보러 별로 안 가.

다민 : 정말? 왜 안 가는데? 영화 보는 거 안 좋아해?

영화 : 영화 보는 건 좋아하지. 하지만 근래 들어서 극장에 가서 보는 건 별로다 싶어서.

다민 : 그래, 어떤 때는 티켓 가격이 너무 비싸지.

영화 : 스낵하고 음료도 너무 비싸.

다민 : 그건 그래. 그래도 극장에서 영화를 감상하는 건 집에서 보는 것과는 좀 다른 기분이지.

영화 : 그렇고 말고. 큰 화면에다, 웅장한 사운드 시스템, 그리고 분위기등이 극장이 훨씬 낫지.

다민 : 어떤 영화는 집에서 봐도 괜찮지만, 가끔씩 영화는 극장에서 봐야 돼.

영화 : 완전 동의. 그런데 시간과 돈이 너무 많이 들어. 사람들이 시끄럽기도 하고.

다민 : 이해가 간다. 그래도 가끔씩은 극장에서 볼 가치가 있어.

영화 : 그런가.

다민 : 극장에서 본 마지막 영화가 뭔데?

영화 : "타이타닉".

다민 : 와! 아주 오래 전 일이네!

영화 : 아니, 그렇지도 않아. 3D 버전은 지난 달에 나왔지? 여기 내 휴대 폰에 그 사진이 있는 걸!

22. 영화 재미있었어?

영화 : 어제 밤에 본 영화 어땠어?

다민 : ____

영화 : 난 영화 보러 자주는 안 가.

다민 : ____

영화 : 영화 보는 건 좋아하지. 하지만 근래 들어서 극장에 가서 보는 건 어떨까 해서.

다민 : ____

영화 : 스낵하고 음료도 너무 비싸.

다민 : ____

영화 : 그렇구 말구, 큰 화면에다, 멋진 사운드 시스템, 그리고 분위기등이 극장이 훨씬 낫지.

다민 : ____

영화 : 그 점에 대해서는 나도 동의해. 그런데 때때로 시간과 돈이 너무 많이 들어. 사람들이
시끄럽기도 하고.

다민 : ____

영화 : 그건 그래.

다민 : ____

영화 : "타이타닉".

다민 : ____

영화 : 아니, 그렇지도 않아. **3D** 버전은 지난 달에 나왔지? 여기 내 휴대 폰에 그 사진이 있는 걸!

22. 영화 재미있었어?

영화 : ____

다민 : 아, 그거 정말 좋더라. 너도 가서 봐.

영화 : ____

다민 : 정말? 왜 안 가는데? 영화 보는 거 안 좋아해?

영화 : ____

다민 : 그래, 어떤 때는 티켓 가격이 너무 비싸지.

영화 : ____

다민 : 그건 사실이야. 그래도 극장에서 영화를 감상하는 건 집에서 보는 것과는 좀 다른

기분이지.

영화 : ____

다민 : 어떤 영화는 집에서 봐도 괜찮지만, 가끔씩 영화는 극장에서 봐야 돼.

영화 : ____

다민 : 이해가 간다. 그래도 가끔씩은 극장에서 볼 가치가 있어.

영화 : ____

다민 : 극장에서 본 마지막 영화가 뭔데?

영화 : ____

다민 :와! 아주 오래 전 일이네!

영화 : ____

MY NOTES:

23.	What's your exercise goal?

Damin : Are you still working out these days?

Dahyeon: Yes, but not as much as before.

Damin : Really? Why's that?

Dahyeon: Well, my exercise goals have changed.

Damin : Oh, so you reached your goals already.

Dahyeon: Not completely.

Damin : What do you mean?

Dahyeon: I had different goals.

Damin : Like what?

Dahyeon: I had goals to workout 5 days per week, to gain muscle, and to lose 10 kilos.

Damin : Those seem like pretty good goals, and maybe not too difficult.

Dahyeon: Yeah, I hit those goals after a few weeks.

Damin : So, you lost your motivation?

Dahyeon: You might say that.

Damin : Was there something else?

Dahyeon: Yes, there was a girl at the gym I wanted to impress.

Damin : Ah… I see…

Dahyeon: So that was one of my other goals.

Damin : But you didn't reach that goal?

Dahyeon: No, it didn't work out.

Damin : What happened? Did she say "no" when you asked her out?

Dahyeon: No, the day I hit my weight loss goal I went to ask her, and she introduced me to her boyfriend. He's the owner of the gym.

23. 운동하는 목표가 뭐지?

다민 : 요즘도 여전히 운동하고 있어?

다현 : 그래, 하지만 예전 같이 많이는 안 해.

다민 : 정말? 왜 안 해?

다현 : 그러게, 내 운동의 목표가 바뀌었어.

다민 : 아, 예전에 하던 운동 목표는 이미 달성했구나.

다현 : 완전히 달성한 건 아니구.

다민 : 무슨 뜻이야?

다현 : 특별한 목표가 있었어.

다민 : 어떤 목표?

다현 : 주 5일 씩 운동해서 근육은 키우고, **10** 킬로그램은 **뺀**다는 거.

다민 : 꽤 훌륭한 목표 같은데? 너무 어렵지도 않은 거 같고.

다현 : 그래, 몇 주 후에는 내가 그 목표를 달성했어.

다민 : 그래서, 이제 운동에 대한 의욕을 잃어 버린 거야?

다현 : 그렇다고도 말 할 수 있어.

다민 : 다른 무슨 이유가 있었어?

다현 : 그래, 그 체육관에 아주 맘에 드는 여자애가 하나 있었거든.

다민 : 아~! 알겠다.

다현 : 그 애가 내가 운동하는 다른 목표 중의 하나였거든.

다민 : 그런데 그 목표는 달성이 안 됐구나?

다현 : 아니, 달성 못 했어.

다민 : 어떻게 됐는데? 네가 사귀자고 하니까 "No"라고 대답했어?

다현 : 아니, 내 체중 감량 목표가 달성되던 날, 내가 그 여자애에게 고백을 했거든. 그랬더니 그 애가 제 남친을 소개하더라. 그 사람이 그 체육관의 오너였어.

23. 운동 목표가 뭐지?

다민 : 요즘도 여전히 운동하고 있어?

다현 : ____

다민 : 정말? 왜?

다현 : ____

다민 : 아, 예전의 운동 목표는 이미 달성했구나.

다현 : ____

다민 : 무슨 뜻이야?

다현 : ____

다민 : 어떤 목표?

다현 : ____

다민 : 꽤 훌륭한 목표 같은데? 너무 어렵지도 않고.

다현 : ____

다민 : 그래서, 이제 운동의 의욕을 잃어 버린거구나?

다현 : ____

다민 : 달리 무슨 이유라도 있었어?

다현 : ____

다민 : 아! 알겠다.

다현 : ____

다민 : 그런데 그 목표는 달성이 안 됐구나?

다현 : ____

다민 : 어떻게 됐는데? 네가 사귀자고 하니까 "No"라고 대답했어?

다현 : ____

23. 운동 목표가 뭐지?

다민 : ＿＿＿＿＿＿＿＿＿＿＿＿＿＿＿＿＿＿＿＿＿＿

다현 : 그래, 하지만 예전 같이는 안 해.

다민 : ＿＿＿＿＿＿＿＿＿＿＿＿＿＿＿＿＿＿＿＿＿＿

다현 : 글쎄, 내 운동 목표가 바뀌었어.

다민 : ＿＿＿＿＿＿＿＿＿＿＿＿＿＿＿＿＿＿＿＿＿＿

다현 : 완전히 달성한 건 아니구.

다민 : ＿＿＿＿＿＿＿＿＿＿＿＿＿＿＿＿＿＿＿＿＿＿

다현 : 특별한 목표가 있었어.

다민 : ＿＿＿＿＿＿＿＿＿＿＿＿＿＿＿＿＿＿＿＿＿＿

다현 : 일주일에 5일 씩 운동해서 근육은 키우고, **10** 킬로그램은 뺀다는 거.

다민 : ＿＿＿＿＿＿＿＿＿＿＿＿＿＿＿＿＿＿＿＿＿＿

다현 : 그래, 몇 주 후에는 내가 그 목표를 달성했지.

다민 : ＿＿＿＿＿＿＿＿＿＿＿＿＿＿＿＿＿＿＿＿＿＿

다현 : 그렇다고도 말 할 수 있어.

다민 : v

다현 : 응, 그 체육관에 아주 맘에 드는 여자애가 하나 있었거든.

다민 : ＿＿＿＿＿＿＿＿＿＿＿＿＿＿＿＿＿＿＿＿＿＿

다현 : 그 애가 내 운동의 또 다른 목표 중의 하나였었거든.

다민 : ＿＿＿＿＿＿＿＿＿＿＿＿＿＿＿＿＿＿＿＿＿＿

다현 : 아니, 달성 못 했어.

다민 : ＿＿＿＿＿＿＿＿＿＿＿＿＿＿＿＿＿＿＿＿＿＿

다현 : 아니, 내 체중 감량 목표가 달성된 날, 내가 그 애에게 고백을 했거든. 그랬더니 그 애가 제 남친을 소개해 주더라. 그는 체육관의 소유자입니다.

MY NOTES:

41

24.   Is that a new shirt?

Damin : You look nice today.

Dahyeon: Thanks. But does that mean I don't usually look nice?

Damin : No, no! It's just that you look especially nice today.

Dahyeon: It's okay. I'm just joking.

Damin : Is that a new shirt?

Dahyeon: Yes, it is.

Damin : That style suits you very well.

Dahyeon: Really? Thanks.

Damin : That color too is very good for you.

Dahyeon: Well, do you really think so?

Damin : Oh, sure. It really looks good.

Dahyeon: I'm glad to hear you say that.

Damin : Why? It's true.

Dahyeon: Would this color suit you?

Damin : hmmm, maybe. But usually I prefer lighter colors.

Dahyeon: Are you sure?

Damin : Uh, yes. Did I say something wrong?

Dahyeon: No, no…

Damin : What's in the bag?

Dahyeon: uh… nothing...

Damin : Come on. What's in there?

Dahyeon: Well, it's a shirt just like this one.

Damin : You bought two?

Dahyeon: Yes, this was going to be your birthday present.

Damin : Oh! In that case, the color is great!

24. 새로 산 셔츠야?

다민 : 오늘 참 멋져 보인다.

다현 : 고마워. 그런데 그 말은 평상시의 난 안 멋져 보인다는 뜻이야?

다민 : 아니, 아니! 오늘은 특히 더 멋지다 이거지.

다현 : 괜찮아. 그냥 농담하는 거야.

다민 : 새로 산 셔츠야?

다현 : 응, 그래.

다민 : 그 스타일 네게 참 잘 어울린다.

다현 : 정말? 고마워.

다민 : 그 색깔도 너한테 참 잘 어울리고.

다현 : 응, 정말 그렇게 생각해?

다민 : 그래, 그래. 정말이지 멋져 보여.

다현 : 그렇게 얘기해 주니까 좋네.

다민 : 왜? 사실을 얘기하는 것 뿐이야.

다현 : 이 색깔 네게는 어울릴 거 같애?

다민 : 흐음, 어쩜 어울릴지도. 그래도 난 평상시에는 좀 더 옅은 색을 좋아하지.

다현 : 정말 그래?

다민 : 응, 그래. 내가 뭐 잘못 말했어?

다현 : 아니, 아니.

다민 : 그 봉투에 든 건 뭐야?

다현 : 어 ... 아무것도 아니야.

다민 : 한 번 보자. 거기 뭐가 들어있는데?

다현 : 응, 그냥 셔츠 한 장, 이것과 똑 같은 거.

다민 : 두 장 샀어?

다현 : 그래, 네 생일 선물로 산 건데.

다민 : 아! 그랬구나. 그럼 이 색깔이 최고다!

24. 새로 산 셔츠야?

다민 : 오늘 참 멋져 보인다.

다현 : ____

다민 : 아니, 아니! 오늘은 특히 더 멋지다 이거지.

다현 : ____

다민 : 새로 산 셔츠야?

다현 : ____

다민 : 그 스타일 네게 아주 잘 어울린다, 야.

다현 : ____

다민 : 그 색깔도 너한테 참 잘 어울리고.

다현 : ____

다민 : 응, 그래. 정말이지 멋져 보여.

다현 : ____

다민 : 왜? 사실을 얘기하는 것 뿐이야.

다현 : ____

다민 : 음, 어쩌면. 그래도 난 평상시에는 좀 더 옅은 색을 좋아하지.

다현 : ____

다민 : 응, 그래. 내가 뭐 잘못 말했어?

다현 : ____

다민 : 그 봉투에 든 건 뭐야?

다현 : ____

다민 : 한 번 보자. 거기에 뭐가 들어있는데?

다현 : ____

다민 : 두 장 샀어?

다현 : ____

다민 : 아! 그랬구나. 그럼 이 색깔이 최고다!

24. 새로 산 셔츠야?

다민 : ____

다현 : 고마워. 그런데 그 말은 평상시의 난 멋져 보이지 않는다는 뜻이야?

다민 : ____

다현 : 괜찮아. 그냥 농담하는 거야.

다민 : ____

다현 : 응, 그래.

다민 : ____

다현 : 정말? 고마워.

다민 : ____

다현 : 응, 정말 그렇게 생각해?

다민 : ____

다현 : 그렇게 얘기해 주니까 기쁘네.

다민 : ____

다현 : 이 색깔 네게는 어울릴 거 같애?

다민 : ____

다현 : 정말 그래?

다민 : ____

다현 : 아니, 아니.

다민 : ____

다현 : 어 … 아무것도 …

다민 : ____

다현 : 응, 그냥 셔츠 한 장, 이것과 똑 같은 거.

다민 : ____

다현 : 그래, 네 생일 선물로.

다민 : ____

25.   Can you play the guitar?

Damin : Is that your guitar?

Dahyeon: Yes, of course.

Damin : I didn't know you could play guitar.

Dahyeon: Well, I'm just a beginner.

Damin : Oh? How long have you been playing?

Dahyeon: About 9 months.

Damin : Are you taking lessons?

Dahyeon: I was just playing with a friend, but I started with a teacher 2 months ago.

Damin : I see. How is it going?

Dahyeon: So far, so good. Playing with my friend was more fun, but taking lessons is helping me more.

Damin : In what way?

Dahyeon: My friend and I played songs he taught me.

Damin : But your teacher?

Dahyeon: He is teaching me more about music in general.

Damin : That can be fun, too.

Dahyeon: Yes, but it's more like studying.

Damin : Well, you can do both, right?

Dahyeon: That's true. Sometimes I still play with my friend.

Damin : Good for you!

Dahyeon: Do you play any instruments?

Damin : Sure! All of them!

Dahyeon: Wow! Really?

Damin : Sure. Here in my CD player.

25. 기타 칠 줄 알아?

다민 : 이 기타, 네 거야?

다현 : 그럼, 내 거지.

다민 : 기타 칠 줄 아는지 몰랐는데.

다현 : 응, 아직 초보자야.

다민 : 응? 시작한지 얼마나 됐는데?

다현 : 거의 9개월.

다민 : 레슨 받고 있어?

다현 : 그냥 친구랑 치다가, 2 개월 전부터 선생님한테 배우기 시작했어.

다민 : 그랬구나. 레슨은 잘 돼 가?

다현 : 지금까지는 잘 돼 가는 거 같아. 내 친구하고 기타치는 게 더 재미있기는 하지만 레슨이
도움은 더 많이 돼.

다민 : 어떤 식으로 도움이 돼?

다현 : 내 친구하고는 그 친구가 가르쳐 준 노래를 그냥 쳐 보는 거고.

다민 : 선생님 레슨에서는?

다현 : 일반적인 음악에 대해서 더 많이 가르쳐 줘.

다민 : 그것도 재미있겠는데.

다현 : 그래, 그런데 뭔가 공부를 하고 있다는 느낌이야.

다민 : 그래도 양쪽 다 하지, 그지?

다현 : 그래. 아직도 간혹 내 친구하고 기타치기도 하거든.

다민 : 잘 됐네!

다현 : 넌 무슨 악기 연주해?

다민 : 악기 연주! 악기라는 악기는 모두 다 연주해!

다현 : 우와! 정말이야?

다민 : 그래. 여기 내 CD플레이어로.

25. 기타 칠 줄 알어?

다민 : 기타, 네 거야?

다현 : ____

다민 : 기타 칠 줄 아는지 몰랐는데.

다현 : ____

다민 : 응? 시작한지 얼마나 됐는데?

다현 : ____

다민 : 레슨 받고 있어?

다현 : ____

다민 : 그랬구나. 레슨은 어때?

다현 : ____

다민 : 어떤 방법으로?

다현 : ____

다민 : 선생님의 레슨에서는?

다현 : ____

다민 : 그거 재미있겠는데.

다현 : ____

다민 : 그런데, 양쪽 다 하지, 그지?

다현 : ____

다민 : 잘 됐네!

다현 : ____

다민 : 그럼! 악기라는 악기는 모두 다!

다현 : ____

다민 : 그래. 여기 있는 내 **CD**플레이어로.

25. 기타 칠 줄 알아?

다민 : ____

다현 : 그럼, 내 거지.

다민 : ____

다현 : 응, 아직 초보자야.

다민 : ____

다현 : 거의 9개월.

다민 : ____

다현 : 그냥 친구랑 치다가, 2 개월 전부터 선생님한테 배우기 시작했어.

다민 : ____

다현 : 지금까지는 괜찮은 거 같애. 내 친구와 놀기가 더 재미 있었지만 수업을 받는 것이 나를 더 잘 돕고 있습니다.

다민 : ____

다현 : 내 친구랑은 친구가 가르쳐 준 노래를 그냥 쳐 보는 거고.

다민 : ____

다현 : 일반적으로 음악에 대해서 더 많이 가르쳐 줘.

다민 : ____

다현 : 응, 그런데 뭐 공부하고 있는 느낌이야.

다민 : ____

다현 : 그래. 아직도 간혹 내 친구하고 치기도 하거든.

다민 : ____

다현 : 넌 무슨 악기 연주해?

다민 : ____

다현 : 와! 정말?

다민 : ____

MY NOTES:

26.   Do you know what that is?

Hyocheol : Hey, enjoying your lunch?

Younghwa: Yes. Did you eat?

Hyocheol : Not yet, but soon.

Younghwa: We don't have much time left, you know?

Hyocheol : I know. Oh! What's that?

Younghwa: What?

Hyocheol : Over there.

Younghwa: Over where?

Hyocheol : There. Way behind you.

Younghwa: I don't see anything.

Hyocheol : Look more closely.

Younghwa: I'm trying, but I still don't know what you're talking about.

Hyocheol : Really? It's right there. Straight behind you.

Younghwa: Straight behind me?

Hyocheol : Yes, and a little to the right.

Younghwa: Ah… Do you mean that tall building?

Hyocheol : On the left side of that tall building.

Younghwa: That? That's nothing.

Hyocheol : What is it then?

Younghwa: It's a banner that says there's a big sale.

Hyocheol : Oh? Is that all?

Younghwa: I think so. Hey! Where's my lunch?

Hyocheol : mmmmm mmmm I don't know…

26. 저게 뭐지?

효철 : 이 봐, 점심 먹고 있어?

영화 : 응. 너는 먹었어?

효철 : 아직 안 먹었어, 하지만 곧 먹을 거야.

영화 : 점심 시간 별로 안 남았는데, 알고 있지?

효철 : 알고 있어. 어! 저게 뭐야?

영화 : 뭐 말이야?

효철 : 저~기 저쪽.

영화 : 저기 어디?

효철 : 저기. 네 뒤 편의 저~기.

영화 : 난 아무 것도 안 보여.

효철 : 좀 더 자세히 봐.

영화 : 자세히 보고 있는데. 그래도 네가 뭘 애기하는지 전혀 모르겠어.

효철 : 정말? 바로 저기. 바로 네 뒤 쪽.

영화 : 바로 네 뒤 쪽?

효철 : 그래, 그리고 다시 조금 오른 쪽.

영화 : 아 ... 저 큰 건물을 가리키는 거야?

효철 : 그 큰 건물의 왼 편.

영화 : 저거? 아무것도 아니야.

효철 : 뭔데, 그럼!

영화 : 대할인판매를 한다는 깃발들이야.

효철 : 아? 그냥 그거 뿐이야?

영화 : 그래. 이 봐! 내 점심은 다 어디로 갔지?

효철 : 흐음 흐음, 난 모르는 일이야.

26. 저게 뭐지?

효철 : 이 봐, 점심 먹고 있어?

영화 : ____

효철 : 아직 안 먹었어, 하지만 곧 먹을 거야.

영화 : ____

효철 : 응, 알아. 어! 저게 뭐야?

영화 : ____

효철 : 저~기.

영화 : ____

효철 : 저기. 너 뒤 편의 저~기.

영화 : ____

효철 : 좀 더 자세히 봐.

영화 : ____

효철 : 정말? 바로 저기. 바로 네 뒤쪽.

영화 : ____

효철 : 그리고, 다시 조금 오른쪽.

영화 : ____

효철 : 그 큰 건물의 왼쪽.

영화 : ____

효철 : 뭔데, 그럼!

영화 : ____

효철 : 아? 그거 뿐이야?

영화 : ____

효철 : 흐음 흐음, 난 모르는 일이야.

26. 저게 뭐지?

효철 : ____

영화 : 응. 너는 먹었어?

효철 : ____

영화 : 점심 시간이 별로 안 남은 거, 알지?

효철 : ____

영화 : 뭔데?

효철 : ____

영화 : 저기 어디?

효철 : ____

영화 : 난 아무 것도 안 보이는데?

효철 : ____

영화 : 자세히 보고 있는데? 그래도 네가 뭘 가리키고 있는지 전혀 모르겠어.

효철 : ____

영화 : 바로 네 뒤쪽?

효철 : ____

영화 : 아 ... 저 큰 건물을 가리키는 거야?

효철 : ____

영화 : 저거? 아무것도 아니야.

효철 : ____

영화 : 대 할인 판매를 한다는 깃발들이야.

효철 : ____

영화 : 그래. 이 봐! 내 점심은 다 어디로 갔지?

효철 : ____

27.   Do you like sports?

Damin : Do you like sports?

Dahyeon: Yeah, sure.

Damin : What kinds of sports do you like?

Dahyeon: Oh, I like most pro sports; baseball, basketball, football.

Damin : Football? What about soccer?

Dahyeon: I like playing soccer, but except for big matches like the World Cup I don't watch much.

Damin : Oh? I like to watch a lot of sports. I even watch high school and college games sometimes.

Dahyeon: Do you play any sports?

Damin : I sometimes play basketball. It's easy because I can play alone or with only 1 or 2 others.

Dahyeon: I know! I want to play baseball, but it's really hard to have the space, time, and enough people to play.

Damin : That's so true. You should play more basketball.

Dahyeon: I guess. But I want to play baseball.

Damin : I know an easy way to do that.

Dahyeon: Really? What is it?

Damin : It's very simple, get video games.

Dahyeon: Ah... but it's not the same.

Damin : Still, it's more fun than studying!

Dahyeon: That's right. Let's play now!

27. 스포츠 좋아해?

다민 : 스포츠 좋아해?

다현 : 그럼, 좋아하지.

다민 : 어떤 스포츠 좋아해?

다현 : 음, 야구, 농구, 미식 축구, 프로 스포츠는 거의 다 좋아해.

다민 : 미식 축구? 축구는 안 좋아해?

다현 : 축구를 하는 건 좋아하지만 별로 보지는 않아. 월드컵과 같은 큰 경기를 제외하고는 말야.

다민 : 그래? 나는 스포츠를 아주 많이 봐. 어떤 때는 고등학교끼리의 시합, 대학교끼리의 시합도 봐.

다현 : 직접 하는 스포츠는 없어?

다민 : 가끔 농구를 해. 혼자서 할 수도 있고 또는 한 두 사람, 다른 사람들이 있어도 함께 플레이할 수 있으니까 손쉽게 하지.

다현 : 그래! 나는 야구가 더 좋아. 그런데 할려면 장소나 시간, 그리고 플레이할 수 있는 인원수를 모으기가 정말 힘들어.

다민 : 정말 그래. 농구를 좀 더 해 보는 게 어때.

다현 : 그렇게 해 볼까. 그래도 난 야구가 더 하고 싶어.

다민 : 간단하게 야구할 수 있는 방법 하나 알려 줄까.

다현 : 정말이야? 어떻게 하는데 ?

다민 : 아주 간단해, 비디오 게임으로 해.

다현 : 음... 하지만 직접하는 거와는 다르지.

다민 : 그래도, 그렇게 하는 게 공부하는 거보다는 더 재미있잖아!

다현 : 하긴 그래. 그럼 당장 시작해 보자!

27. 스포츠 좋아하세요?

다민 : 스포츠 좋아하세요?

다현 : ____

다민 : 어떤 스포츠 좋아하시는데요?

다현 : ____

다민 : 미식 축구? 축구는 안 좋아해요?

다현 : ____

다민 : 그래요? 나는 스포츠를 많이 봅니다. 어떤 때는 고등학교 별 시합, 대학 별 시합도
보는데요.

다현 : ____

다민 : 가끔 농구를 해요. 혼자서도 할 수 있고 또는 한 두 사람, 다른 사람들이 있어도 함께
플레이 할 수 있기 때문에 아주 손쉬워요.

다현 : ____

다민 : 정말 그래요. 농구를 좀 더 하시지 그래요.

다현 : ____

다민 : 간단하게 할 수 있는 방법을 하나 알려 드릴까요.

다현 : ____

다민 : 아주 간단해요, 비디오 게임으로 하는 거예요.

다현 : ____

다민 : 그래도, 공부하는 거보다는 더 재미있지 않아요!

다현 : ____

27. 스포츠 좋아하세요?

다민 : ____

다현 : 네, 그럼요.

다민 : ____

다현 : 음, 프로 스포츠는 거의 다 좋아해요. 야구, 농구, 미식 축구.

다민 : ____

다현 : 축구 하는 건 좋아하지만 별로 보지는 않습니다. 월드컵과 같은 큰 경기를 제외하고는요.

다민 : ____

다현 : 직접 하는 스포츠는 없나요?

다민 : ____

다현 : 그렇죠! 나는 야구가 하고 싶은데, 할려면 장소라든지 시간이라든지, 또는 플레이할 수
있는 인명수를 모으기가 정말 힘들어요.

다민 : ____

다현 : 그게 쉽겠네요. 그래도 난 야구가 더 하고 싶어요.

다민 : ____

다현 : 정말요? 그게 뭔데요?

다민 : ____

다현 : 음... 하지만 직접하는 거와는 다르죠.

다민 : ____

다현 : 그건 사실이에요. 지금 당장 시작해 봅시다!

28.	How was last night?

Hyocheol : So, how was last night?

Younghwa: It was great.

Hyocheol : That's good.

Younghwa: It was even better than I thought it would be.

Hyocheol : Really. That's very good since I know how much you were looking forward to going.

Younghwa: I know. I was worried I might be disappointed, but I wasn't.

Hyocheol : That happens to me a lot with movies.

Younghwa: I didn't know you were a big movie fan.

Hyocheol : I'm not really, but some movies I get really excited about. And then I worry they won't be as good as I thought.

Younghwa: Oh, I understand. That kind of thing happens to me a lot.

Hyocheol : Oh? You're a big movie fan, too?

Younghwa: Sometimes, But that's not the thing that worries me the most.

Hyocheol : Then what do you worry about disappointing you?

Younghwa: Lunch!

Hyocheol : Everything with you is about food!

Younghwa: No, it's not. Sometimes it's movies.

Hyocheol : Like what?

Younghwa: uh… Ratatouille.

28. 어제 밤은 어땠어?

효철 : 그래, 어제 밤은 어땠어?

영화 : 아주 좋았어.

효철 : 잘 됐네.

영화 : 내가 기대했던 것보다 더 멋지던 걸.

효철 : 정말이야? 진짜 잘 됐네. 가기 전부터 잔뜩 기대를 하고 있었잖아.

영화 : 그래. 난 실망하게 될까 봐 걱정했었는데 그게 아니었어.

효철 : 난 영화 보러 갈 때는 그런 실망을 당할 때가 많아.

영화 : 그만큼 영화를 좋아하는 영화 팬인줄은 몰랐는데?

효철 : 그리 대단한 팬은 아니고. 그래도 어떤 영화에 대해서는 정말 기대를 많이 하게 되지. 그러면서 내가 기대한 만큼 안 좋으면 어떻게 하나 걱정도 하면서.

영화 : 응, 이해가 가. 나도 그런 일이 많이 있어.

효철 : 응? 너도 대단한 영화 팬이야?

영화 : 때로는 그래. 그런데 내가 가장 걱정하는 건 그런 게 아냐.

효철 : 그럼 네가 가장 실망하게 되는 건 뭔데?

영화 : 점심!

효철 : 넌 뭐든지 다 먹는 거하고 연결되는구나!

영화 : 아니, 그런 건 아니고. 간혹은 영화에 대해서 실망하기도 해.

효철 : 어떤 거?

영화 : 음 ... 영화 라따뚜이.

28. 어제 밤에는 어땠어?

효철 : 그래, 어제 밤에는 어땠어?

영화 : ____

효철 : 잘 됐네.

영화 : ____

효철 : 정말? 진짜 잘 됐네. 네가 가기 전부터 잔뜩 기대를 하고 있었잖아.

영화 : ____

효철 : 난 그런 일을 많이 당하지. 영화에 있어서는 말야.

영화 : ____

효철 : 그리 대단한 팬은 아니고. 그래도 어떤 영화에 대해서는 정말 기대를 많이 하게 되지.
그러면서 내가 생각했던 기대치만큼 안 좋으면 어떻게 하나 걱정도 하고.

영화 : ____

효철 : 응? 너도 대단한 영화 팬이었지?

영화 : ____

효철 : 그럼 네가 가장 실망하게 되는 건 뭔데?

영화 : ____

효철 : 넌 뭐든지 다 식사하고 연결되는구나!

영화 : ____

효철 : 어떤 거?

영화 : ____

28. 어제 밤에는 어땠어?

효철 : ____

영화 : 아주 좋았어.

효철 : ____

영화 : 내가 기대하고 있던 것보다 더 낫던 걸.

효철 : ____

영화 : 그래. 난 실망하게 될까 봐 걱정했었는데 그게 아니었어.

효철 : ____

영화 : 네가 그만큼 영화를 좋아하는 영화 팬인줄은 몰랐는데?

효철 : ____

영화 : 응, 이해가 가. 나도 그런 일이 많이 있지.

효철 : ____

영화 : 응, 꽤나. 그런데 내가 가장 걱정하는 건 그런 게 아냐.

효철 : ____

영화 : 점심!

효철 : ____

영화 : 아니, 그런 건 아니고. 간혹은 영화에 대해서 실망하기도 하지.

효철 : ____

영화 : 음 ... 영화 라따뚜이.

MY NOTES:

29.   I can't live without my computer!

Damin : You are always studying these days.

Dahyeon: What?

Damin : Every time I see you it looks like you are working hard on your computer.

Dahyeon: I guess it could look that way.

Damin : You must be doing a lot better in school.

Dahyeon: Well, I have gotten a lot better at typing.

Damin : That's important.

Dahyeon: Yes, and my spelling is also better.

Damin : Computers are very good for helping you to spell and write better.

Dahyeon: Yes, it gets easier all the time.

Damin : What subjects are you studying the most on your computer?

Dahyeon: I'm studying many, many subjects these days.

Damin : Like what? Science? History? Literature?

Dahyeon: Actually it's more like sports, movies, and entertainment.

Damin : Really? Those are classes you are taking?

Dahyeon: Not actually.

Damin : What are they then?

Dahyeon: They're the things my friends and I talk about every day on Facebook.

29. 컴퓨터 없이는 살 수 없어!

다민 : 요즘 늘 공부하고 있네.

다현 : 뭐라구?

다민 : 너 볼 때마다 컴퓨터로 열심히 공부하고 있는 것 같이 보이는데?

다현 : 그게 그렇게 보일 수도 있겠네.

다민 : 학교 공부도 많이 좋아졌지?

다현 : 글쎄, 타이핑하는 실력은 훨씬 많이 좋아졌어.

다민 : 그게 중요한 거잖아.

다현 : 그래, 내 철자법도 좀 좋아졌어.

다민 : 컴퓨터가 철자법 및 작문 실력 향상에 아주 좋은 도움이 되는 것 같애.

다현 : 그래, 할 때마다 좀 더 쉬워지는 것 같아.

다민 : 컴퓨터로는 어떤 과목을 제일 열심히 공부하는 거야?

다현 : 요즘은 아주 많은 과목들을 공부하는 중이야.

다민 : 어떤 과목? 과학? 역사? 문학?

다현 : 실은, 스포츠, 영화, 그리고 오락 같은 게 더 많아.

다민 : 정말? 그런 과목들을 공부하고 있다구?

다현 : 진짜는 그게 아냐.

다민 : 그럼 그것들은 다 뭐야?

다현 : 내 친구하고 내가 매일 페북에서 나누는 이야기들 내용.

29. 컴퓨터 없이는 살 수 없다!

다민 : 요즈음 늘 공부하고 있네.

다현 : ____

다민 : 너 볼 때마다 컴퓨터로 열심히 공부하고 있는 것 같이 보이는데?

다현 : ____.

다민 : 학교 공부도 많이 좋아졌지?

다현 : ____

다민 : 그게 중요한 거잖아.

다현 : ____

다민 : 컴퓨터가 철자법 및 작문 실력 향상에 아주 좋은 도움이 되는 것 같애.

다현 : ____

다민 : 컴퓨터로는 어떤 과목을 제일 열심히 공부하는 거야?

다현 : ____

다민 : 어떤 과목? 과학? 역사? 문학?

다현 : ____

다민 : 정말? 그런 과목들을 공부하고 있다구?

다현 : ____

다민 : 그럼 그것들은 다 뭐야?

다현 : ____

29. 컴퓨터 없이는 살 수 없다!

다민 : ____

다현 : 뭐라구?

다민 : ____

다현 : 그게 그렇게 보일 수도 있겠네.

다민 : ____

다현 : 글쎄, 타이핑하는 실력은 훨씬 많이 좋아졌어.

다민 : ____

다현 : 그래, 내 철자법도 좀 좋아졌어.

다민 : ____

다현 : 응, 할 때마다 좀 더 쉬워지는 것 같아.

다민 : ____

다현 : 요즘 여러가지로 많은 과목들을 공부하는 중인데.

다민 : ____

다현 : 실은, 스포츠, 영화에다 오락 같은 게 더 많아.

다민 : ____

다현 : 진짜는 그게 아냐.

다민 : ____

다현 : 내 친구하고 내가 매일 페이스 북에서 나누는 이야기들.

30.   I saw a strange bird!

Hyocheol : You won't believe what I saw on my way here.

Younghwa: Something really strange?

Hyocheol : For me it was.

Younghwa: Well, tell me!

Hyocheol : It was a very strange bird.

Younghwa: A bird?

Hyocheol : Yes.

Younghwa: What kind of bird?

Hyocheol : I'm not sure.

Younghwa: What did it look like?

Hyocheol : It was really fat.

Younghwa: What else?

Hyocheol : It walked funny.

Younghwa: That's not much help.

Hyocheol : It was walking around eating off the ground.

Younghwa: That's not much help either. Most birds do that.

Hyocheol : It was making noises while it ate.

Younghwa: What kind of noises?

Hyocheol : It sounded like "cluck, cluck".

Younghwa: Cluck, cluck?

Hyocheol : Yes, that's what I think it sounded like.

Younghwa: It was just a chicken!

Hyocheol : A chicken?

Younghwa: Yes. You've never seen a chicken before?

Hyocheol : I've only seen them without feathers and in a box!

30. 이상한 새를 봤어!

효철 : 여기 오는 길에 정말 이상한 걸 봤어.

영화 : 정말 이상한 거?

효철 : 그래, 난생 처음 보는 거.

영화 : 어떤 건지 말해 봐!

효철 : 그게 매우 이상하게 생긴 새던데.

영화 : 이상한 새라구?

효철 : 그래.

영화 : 무슨 새?

효철 : 잘 몰라.

영화 : 어떻게 생겼는데?

효철 : 정말 통통하던데….

영화 : 그 외에는?

효철 : 걷는 게 이상했어.

영화 : 별로 도움이 안 되는 정보잖아.

효철 : 흙 위를 걸어다니면서 모이를 쪼고 있었어.

영화 : 그것도 별로 도움이 안 되네. 대부분의 새들이 다 그렇잖아.

효철 : 먹이를 쪼면서 시끄러운 소리를 내던데.

영화 : 어떤 소리?

효철 : 그게 "꼬꼬, 꼬꼬" 하는 거 같았어.

영화 : "꼬꼬, 꼬꼬"?

효철 : 그래, 그런 소리를 내는 것 같이 들렸는데?

영화 : 그건 닭이잖아!

효철 : 닭?

영화 : 그래. 너 이전에 닭 본 적 없어?

효철 : 털도 없이 상자에 들어있는 것만 본 적이 있네!

30. 이상한 새를 봤어!

효철 : 여기 오는 길에 정말 이상한 걸 봤어.

영화 : ____

효철 : 그래, 난생 처음 보는 거.

영화 : ____

효철 : 그게 매우 이상한 새던데.

영화 : ____

효철 : 그래.

영화 : ____

효철 : 잘 몰라.

영화 : ____

효철 : 정말 통통하던데….

영화 : ____

효철 : 걷는 게 이상했어.

영화 : ____

효철 : 흙 위를 걸어다니면서 모이를 쪼고 있었어.

영화 : ____

효철 : 먹이를 쪼면서 시끄러운 소리를 내던데.

영화 : ____

효철 : 그게 "꼬꼬, 꼬꼬" 하는 거 같았어.

영화 : ____

효철 : 그래, 그런 소리를 내는 것 같이 들렸는데?

영화 : ____

효철 : 닭?

영화 : ____

효철 : 털도 없이 상자에 들어있는 것만 본 적이 있네!

30. 이상한 새를 봤어!

효철 : ____

영화 : 정말 이상한 거?

효철 : ____

영화 : 어떤 건지 말해 봐!

효철 : ____

영화 : 이상한 새라구?

효철 : ____

영화 : 무슨 새?

효철 : ____

영화 : 어떻게 생겼는데?

효철 : ____

영화 : 그 외에는?

효철 : ____

영화 : 별로 도움이 안 되는 정보잖아.

효철 : ____

영화 : 그것도 별로 도움이 안 되네. 대부분의 새들이 다 그렇잖아.

효철 : ____

영화 : 어떤 소리?

효철 : ____

영화 : "꼬꼬, 꼬꼬"?

효철 : ____

영화 : 그건 닭이잖아!

효철 : ____

영화 : 그래. 너 이전에 닭 본 적 없지?

효철 : ____

31.　　On a ski trip

Damin : Hey! What happened to your leg!

Dahyeon: Don't you remember? I told you I was going skiing last weekend.

Damin : Yes, but you said you were a good skier.

Dahyeon: Well, yes, that's true.

Damin : You wanted me to try skiing, too.

Dahyeon: Yes, that's also true.

Damin : You said skiing is really fun and not as dangerous as everyone says.

Dahyeon: Yes, I know I said that.

Damin : And you broke your leg?

Dahyeon: Yes, I did.

Damin : So, what do you have to say for yourself about that now?

Dahyeon: I still have the same things to say. Skiing is fun and not as dangerous as everyone says.

Damin : And you still think I should try it?

Dahyeon: Sure, you would love skiing.

Damin : How can you say that? I thought you were my friend.

Dahyeon: I am your friend.

Damin : But you still want me to try skiing.

Dahyeon: Sure. Why not?

Damin : Because you went skiing and broke your leg!

Dahyeon: Oh, I broke my leg rushing to get off the bus at the resort.

31. 스키 여행

다민 : 이 봐! 다리는 어떻게 된거야!

다현 : 생각 나? 지난 주말에 내가 스키 간다고 한 거.

다민 : 응, 하지만 넌 스키를 잘 탄다고 했잖아.

다현 : 어, 그래, 그건 사실이야.

다민 : 나보고도 스키를 한 번 해 보라고 했지.

다현 : 그래, 그것도 사실이야.

다민 : 스키가 정말 재미있고 남들 얘기하는 만큼 위험하지도 않다고 말했지?

다현 : 응, 내가 그렇게 얘기했어.

다민 : 그러고도 넌 다리가 부러졌고?

다현 : 그래, 다리가 부러졌어.

다민 : 그럼, 이제 그것에 대해서 어떻게 설명할래?

다현 : 그래도 똑 같은 말을 할 건데. 스키는 재미있고 남들 얘기하는 만큼 위험하지도 않다고 말야.

다민 : 그리고 아직도 나보고 스키를 한 번 해 보라구?

다현 : 그래, 넌 아마 스키를 아주 좋아하게 될 걸.

다민 : 너 어떻게 그런 말을 할 수 있어? 우리는 친한 친구이면서.

다현 : 그럼 우린 친구지.

다민 : 그런데도 여전히 날더러 스키를 한 번 해 보라고?

다현 : 그럼. 왜 안해?

다민 : 네가 스키 가서 네 다리를 분지르고 왔기 때문이잖아!

다현 : 어 이거? 리조트장에서 버스에서 얼른 내리려다 부러트린 거야.

31. 스키 여행

다민 : 이 봐! 다리는 어떻게 된거야!

다현 : ____

다민 : 응, 하지만 넌 스키를 잘 탄다고 했잖아.

다현 : ____

다민 : 나보고도 스키를 한 번 해 보라고 했지.

다현 : ____

다민 : 스키가 정말 재미있고 다들 얘기되어지는 만큼 위험하지도 않다고 말했지?

다현 : ____

다민 : 그러고도 넌 다리가 부러졌고?

다현 : ____.

다민 : 그럼, 이제 그것에 대해서 어떻게 설명할래?

다현 : ____

다민 : 그리고 아직도 나보고 스키를 한 번 해 보라구?

다현 : ____

다민 : 너 어떻게 그런 말을 할 수 있어? 우리는 진실한 친구이면서.

다현 : ____

다민 : 그런데도 여전히 날더러 스키를 한 번 해 보라고?

다현 : ____

다민 : 네가 스키 가서 네 다리를 분지르고 왔기 때문이잖아!

다현 : ____

31. 스키 여행

다민 : ____

다현 : 생각나? 지난 주말에 내가 스키 간다고 한 거.

다민 : ____

다현 : 어, 그래, 그건 사실이야.

다민 : ____

다현 : 그래, 그것도 사실이야.

다민 : ____

다현 : 응, 내가 그렇게 얘기했지.

다민 : ____

다현 : 그래, 다리가 부러졌어.

다민 : ____

다현 : 그래도 똑 같은 말을 할건데. 스키는 재미있고 다들 얘기되어지는 만큼 위험하지도 않다고 말야.

다민 : ____

다현 : 그래, 넌 아마 스키를 아주 좋아하게 될 걸.

다민 : ____

다현 : 그럼 우린 친구지.

다민 : ____

다현 : 그럼. 왜 안해?

다민 : ____

다현 : 어 이거? 리조트장에서 버스에서 서둘러 하차하면서 부러트린 거야.

81

32.   There's a new coffee shop you should try.

Hyocheol : Did you hear about the new coffee shop?

Younghwa: New coffee shop? No. Where?

Hyocheol : It's over by the Indonesian restaurant.

Younghwa: Indonesian restaurant? I don't even know where that is.

Hyocheol : Really?

Younghwa: How far is that from here?

Hyocheol : It's not so far. If you have time, you can walk there.

Younghwa: How long does it take?

Hyocheol : If you walk a little fast, it takes about 20 minutes.

Younghwa: 20 minutes? How do you get there?

Hyocheol : Just go straight up this street to the department store.

Younghwa: All the way to the department store? Ok. After that?

Hyocheol : Then turn right and go 3 blocks and turn left.

Younghwa: Turn right, then left after 3 blocks.

Hyocheol : Yes, then go 1 block and turn left again.

Younghwa: 1 block, then left.

Hyocheol : Then go to the convenience store and turn right.

Younghwa: Wow. Is that it?

Hyocheol : You still have to turn right again at the cleaners.

Younghwa: I don't think I can remember all that. Is there an easier way?

Hyocheol : I only know that way. Can you find it?

Younghwa: Oh, sure. I'll take a taxi!

32. 새로 생긴 커피 숍

효철 : 새로 생긴 커피 숍 얘기 들었어?

영화 : 새로 생긴 커피 숍? 아니, 어디에?

효철 : 인도네시안 레스토랑 건너편 쪽에.

영화 : 인도네시안 레스토랑? 그게 어디 있는지도 모르는데.

효철 : 정말 몰라?

영화 : 여기에서 얼마나 걸리는데?

효철 : 그렇게 멀지는 않아. 시간만 있으면, 걸어 가도 돼.

영화 : 얼마나 걸리는데?

효철 : 조금 빨리 걸어서 약 20 분 정도 걸려.

영화 : 20 분? 어떻게 가는데?

효철 : 백화점쪽으로 이 길을 곧장 올라가.

영화 : 백화점까지 그 먼 길을? 좋아. 그러고는?

효철 : 그러고는 오른쪽으로 꺾어서 3 블록을 가서 좌회전.

영화 : 오른쪽으로 꺾어서 3 블록을 가서 좌회전.

효철 : 그래, 그리고 1 블록 가서 다시 좌회전.

영화 : 1 블록 가서 또 좌회전.

효철 : 그러고서 편의점까지 가서 우회전.

영화 : 놀랍다. 그게 전부야?

효철 : 아직 세탁소까지 가서 다시 우회전을 해야 하는데….

영화 : 그걸 어떻게 다 기억해. 좀 쉬운 방법은 없어?

효철 : 내가 아는 길은 이 길 뿐이야. 찾을 수 있어?

영화 : 응, 그래. 나는 택시 탈게!

32. 새로 생긴 커피 숍

효철 : 새로 생긴 커피 숍 얘기 들었어?

영화 : ________________________________

효철 : 인도네시언 레스토랑쪽 저편에.

영화 : ________________________________

효철 : 정말?

영화 : ________________________________

효철 : 그렇게 멀지는 않아. 시간이 있으면, 걸어 가도 돼.

영화 : ________________________________

효철 : 조금 빨리 걸어서 약 **20** 분 정도 걸려.

영화 : ________________________________

효철 : 백화점까지 이 길을 곧장 올라가.

영화 : ________________________________

효철 : 그러고는 오른쪽으로 **3** 블록을 가서 좌회전.

영화 : ________________________________

효철 : 그래, 그리고 한 블록 가서 다시 좌회전.

영화 : ________________________________

효철 : 그러고서 편의점까지 가서 우회전.

영화 : ________________________________

효철 : 아직 세탁소까지 가서 다시 우회전을 해야하는데….

영화 : ________________________________

효철 : 내가 아는 길은 이 길이야. 찾을 수 있어?

영화 : ________________________________

32. 새로 생긴 커피 숍

효철 : ____

영화 : 새로 생긴 커피 숍? 아오, 어디에?

효철 : ____

영화 : 인도네시언 레스토랑? 그게 어디 있는지도 모르는데.

효철 : ____

영화 : 여기에서 얼마나 걸려?

효철 : ____

영화 : 얼마나 걸리는데?

효철 : ____

영화 : 20 분? 어떻게 가는데?

효철 : ____

영화 : 백화점까지 그 먼 길을? 좋아. 그러고는?

효철 : ____

영화 : 오른쪽으로 3 블록을 가서 좌회전.

효철 : ____

영화 : 한 블록 가서 또 좌회전.

효철 : ____

영화 : 와우. 이제는 끝인가?

효철 : ____

영화 : 그걸 다 기억할 수는 없겠네. 좀 쉬운 방법은 없나?

효철 : ____

영화 : 응, 그래. 나는 택시 탈께!

About the authors:

Allen Williams was born and raised in the United States. He graduated from Murray State University with a Bachelors in Broadcast and a Masters in American Literature. He then earned a PhD while living and working in South Korea. He is the author of several textbooks for English language learning as well as for learning Korean. After spending 6 years in Korea, he moved to Japan where he lives with his wife and two sons and teaches at university.

Sulseob Jo was born and raised in South Korea. She graduated from university in South Korea with an undergraduate degree in Chinese characters. She then moved to Japan to study at Nagoya University where she earned a Masters and a PhD in Chinese literature. She is a professor teaching a wide range of subjects from Korean language to Chinese literature as well as Asian culture. She is the author of several books on learning Korean language. She and her husband live in Japan with their two sons.